W9-APB-925

Water Frog Polliwogs

by Dawn Bluemel Oldfield

Consultant:
Mary Rogalski, MESc
Yale University
School of Forestry & Environmental Studies

BEARPORT
PUBLISHING

New York, New York

Credits

Cover and Title Page, © D.R. Schrichte/seapics.com; 4–5, © Doug Wechsler/Nature Picture Library; 6, © Cosmographics; 6–7, © Wildlife GmbH/Alamy; 8, © D.R. Schrichte/seapics. com; 9, © Breck P. Kent/Animals Animals; 11T, © Photo Researchers/FLPA; 11B, © Photo Researchers/FLPA; 12–13, © Wildlife GmbH/Alamy; 14–15, © Dirk Ercken/Shutterstock and © Nature Production/Nature Picture Library; 17, © Photo Researchers/FLPA; 18–19, © Kenneth H. Thomas/Science Photo Library; 20, © Karl R. Martin/Shutterstock; 21, © Gerald Marella/ Shutterstock; 22T, © Wildlife GmbH/Alamy; 22C, © Wikipedia Creative Commons; 22B, © Photo Researchers/FLPA; 23T, © Breck P. Kent/Animals Animals; 23C, © moomsabuy/ Shutterstock; 23B, © Doug Wechsler/Nature Picture Library.

Publisher: Kenn Goin
Editorial Director: Adam Siegel
Creative Director: Spencer Brinker
Design: Emma Randall
Editor: Mark J Sachner
Photo Researcher: Ruby Tuesday Books Ltd

Library of Congress Cataloging-in-Publication Data

Bluemel Oldfield, Dawn
  Water frog polliwogs / by Dawn Bluemel Oldfield.
    p. cm. — (Water babies)
  Includes bibliographical references and index.
  ISBN 978-1-61772-606-4 (library binding) — ISBN 1-61772-606-0 (library binding)
  1. Bullfrog—Life cycles—Juvenile literature. I. Title.
  QL668.E27B59 2013
  597.8′92156—dc23
                    2012012473

For more information, write to Bearport Publishing Company, Inc., 45 West 21st Street, Suite 3B, New York, New York 10010. Printed in the United States of America.

10 9 8 7 6 5 4 3 2 1

Contents

Meet a polliwog

A tiny **polliwog** swims in a pond.

It is looking for plants to eat.

The polliwog looks like a little fish, but it is really a baby American bullfrog.

Very soon it will go through some big changes.

American bullfrog polliwog

All about American bullfrogs

Adult American bullfrogs live near ponds, lakes, and streams.

They spend some time in water and some time on land.

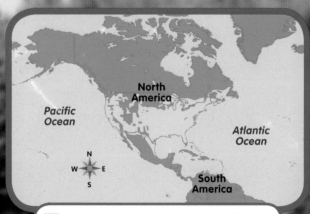

North America

Pacific Ocean

Atlantic Ocean

N
W E
S

South America

Where American bullfrogs live in North America

Bullfrogs are the largest type of frog in North America.

An adult bullfrog can weigh as much as five baseballs!

adult American bullfrog

Bullfrog eggs

A mother bullfrog lays her eggs in a pond or lake.

She lays up to 20,000 eggs at one time.

The eggs look like black dots floating in blobs of clear jelly.

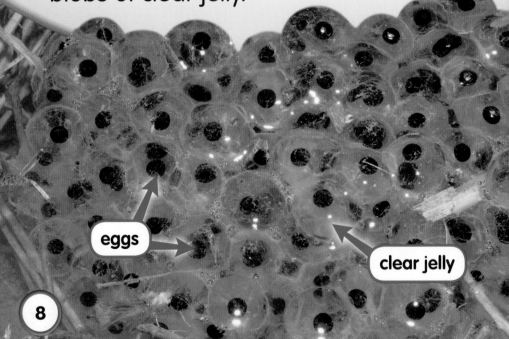

eggs

clear jelly

In about five days, a polliwog, or tadpole, **hatches** from each egg.

Each baby frog is smaller than a dime!

polliwogs

Water babies

A polliwog looks very different from an adult bullfrog.

It has a long tail and no legs.

A polliwog must live in water because, unlike an adult frog, it cannot breathe air.

It can only breathe underwater.

It has body parts called **gills** to help it breathe in water.

two-day-old polliwog

eight-week-old polliwog

tail

the gills are under here

What do polliwogs eat?

Polliwogs spend their days swimming and looking for food.

They eat underwater plants and **algae**.

They have tiny teeth to scrape pieces of algae off of logs and rocks.

Polliwogs eat a lot of food to help them grow.

In a few months, they can grow to be as long as a new pencil!

algae

Big changes

When a polliwog is about a year old, its body begins to change.

It grows back legs and then front legs.

Its tail starts to get shorter, too.

tail

back leg

one-year-old
polliwog

front leg

Growing up

By the time a polliwog is nearly two years old, it looks a lot like a grown-up frog.

It is much smaller than an adult, however.

The polliwog's legs keep growing bigger and its tail keeps getting shorter.

It also grows body parts, called lungs, for breathing air.

Meet a froglet

At two years old, the polliwog has become a young frog called a **froglet**.

It swims in the pond and hops on land using its legs.

It hunts among plants for small animals to eat, such as **insects** and worms.

froglet

worm

Meet a bullfrog

At five years old, the young frog is about six inches (15 cm) long.

It is almost fully grown.

adult bullfrog on land

The young frog is large enough to catch and eat snakes and other frogs.

Now it is ready to begin its life as an adult American bullfrog.

adult bullfrog in water

Glossary

algae (AL-gee)
plant-like living things
that grow in lakes, ponds,
rivers, and oceans

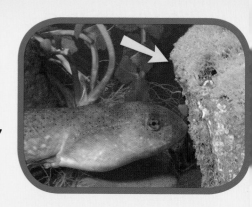

froglet (FROG-lit)
a small, young frog that
is not yet fully grown

gills (GILZ) body parts
that polliwogs and other
underwater animals,
such as fish, use for
breathing

hatches (HACH-iz)
breaks out of an egg

insects (IN-sekts)
small animals that have six legs, three main body parts, two antennas, and a hard shell called an exoskeleton

polliwog (POL-ee-wog)
a baby frog that lives in water; another name for a tadpole

Index

Read more

Carney, Elizabeth. *Frogs! (National Geographic Readers)*. Washington, D.C.: National Geographic (2009).

Lawrence, Ellen. *A Frog's Life (Animal Diaries: Life Cycles)*. New York: Bearport (2012).

Zemlicka, Shannon. *From Tadpole to Frog (Start to Finish)*. Minneapolis, MN: Lerner (2012).

Learn more online

To learn more about frogs, visit
www.bearportpublishing.com/WaterBabies

About the author

Dawn Bluemel Oldfield is a freelance writer. When she isn't writing, she enjoys reading, traveling, and working in her yard. She and her husband live in Prosper, Texas, where she is a master gardener.